SEX IN THE COUNTRY

SEX IN THE COUNTRY

VERY SPORTING CARTOONS BY BRYN PARRY

SWAN·HILL
PRESS

DEDICATION

This book is dedicated to all the chicks, birds, old dogs and lovely little bitches in my life... I just don't know what I would do without you.

The cartoons on pages 113, 114, 115 and 122 are reproduced with kind permission of *The Field*

The cartoon on page 89 is reproduced with kind permission of *Horse & Hound*

The cartoons on pages 90 and 96 are reproduced with kind permission of *The Shooting Gazette*

Copyright © 2005 Bryn Parry

First published in the UK in 2005
by Swan Hill Press, an imprint of Quiller Publishing Ltd

British Library Cataloguing-in-Publication Data
A catalogue record for this book
is available from the British Library

ISBN 1 904057 66 7

Printed in Singapore

Swan Hill Press
an imprint of Quiller Publishing Ltd.
Wykey House, Wykey, Shrewsbury, SY4 1JA, England
Tel: 01939 261616 Fax: 01939 261606
E-mail: info@quillerbooks.com
Website: www.swanhillbooks.com

INTRODUCTION

My youngest daughter calls me a Sad Old Git for producing a book on sex. I have to agree with her; there is nothing sadder than a mature man and his friends sniggering over an inuendo. To think that jokes about cocks, butts and over and unders are funny is not big nor is it clever. In fact, to be able to draw dozens of cartoons based on school-boy humour and worse, to draw titivating pictures of scantily clad ladies is positively disgraceful and I should aplogise profusely...but I won't!

There is nothing tasteful in this book. It is full of purile jokes about the countryside and even includes some quite horrifically Politically Incorrect cartoons about Hunting which are sure to get me locked up...and quite right too.

So there we are, this book is about sex in the country and it is most definately non PC. If you are easily offended or blush when you overhear grown men discussing their birds, then this book is not for you. Put it down now. Shut it and walk away. You have been warned.

If, however, you snigger childishly whenever you hear of a gun looking for his cock, a rider looking for a good mount or a fisherman playing with his tackle, then this is the book for you. It might even be the ideal book for your Granny, your teenage Daughter or your disapproving Aunt; you never know.

Throw caution to the wind, lie back and think of England, relax and enjoy yourself. Brace up and think of Nelson, grit your teeth and get on with it, you never know, you might actually enjoy it.

Bryn Parry

CONTENTS

KEEPER'S TIPS...

FEEDING THE BIRDS

HAND REARED

UNDER KEEPER

11

HEDGE LAYING

COVER CROP

13

A RUNNER

LUNCHTIME ROLL

15

GAME CART

I LIKE A MAN WITH A DECENT LUNCHBOX!

17

A REAL SCREAMER

SIX MILE BOTTOM

19

BLOW JOB

A FEW BIRDS...

BEAUTIFULLY PRESENTED BIRDS

WILD BIRDS

DRESSED BIRD . . .

. . . UNDRESSED BIRD

HIGH BIRD

FLUSHED BIRD

ENGLISHMAN AND REDLEGS

SHARED BIRD

TAKING A BRACE HOME

WOULD YOU LIKE ME TO HOLD YOUR COCK?

THE DEAR OLD DUCK

HALF COCK

COCKS ONLY

SOME DOGS...

WORKING DOG

DOGGY FASHION

THERE'S LIFE IN THE OLD DOG YET

LOVELY LITTLE BITCH

HARD MOUTHED BITCH

COME HERE, YOU SILLY LITTLE BITCH!

THE GUNS..

SHE'S GOT A LOVELY MATCHED PAIR

41

I LOVE A REALLY SMOOTH MOUNT

HE SEEMS TO HAVE A PROBLEM GETTING HIS LEG OVER

NO, WE HAVEN'T SEEN YOUR NIPPLE PRICKER

THE EARLY BIRD GETS THE WORM

STANDING AT STUD

YOUR HUSBAND HAS OFFERED TO POLISH MY BUTT

AVOIDING THE WET PATCH

I'M NOT SURE I REALLY LIKE THESE BIG BAG DAYS

I'M A PHEASANT PLUCKER

50

IN THE BUTTS...

THE LAIRD'S BUTT

HOT BARRELS

ONE IN THE BUTT

SIDE BY SIDE

OVER AND UNDER

GROUSE

HOT ACTION!

I CAN'T WAIT TO GET UNDER SOME REALLY TALL BIRDS

57

DO YOU NEED STUFFING?

PREMATURE EJECTION

THE HOT SEAT

KEEPING THE EYE ON THE BIRD

COMPLETELY OUT OF REACH

BULLOCKS!

BLING BLING!

HE'S GOT A LOVELY PUMP ACTION

WELL PLUCKED

WELL SUPPORTED...

SHOOTING STOCKINGS

POP HOLE

THE BEATER

THE PICKER UP

LOVELY MUFF

NICE WARM BEAVER

THE CARTRIDGE BAG

THE BAG AT THE END OF DAY

THE
AFTERGLOW...

HOT FLUSH

PICKING UP

I NEED A HAND FINDING MY COCK

DON'T MUCK ABOUT … JUST POP THE BREASTS OUT

THAT ONE'S REALLY WELL HUNG

Looking for the pricked Bird

A BIRD IN THE HAND IS WORTH TWO IN THE BUSH

IT WAS AN ENORMOUS COCK UP ACTUALLY

IN SEASON...

THE CRACK OF DAWN

SHORT & CURLY

LAMPING BUNNIES

BIG BANG

PULL!

Hot Shot

THE LIMO LADETTE

GAME FAIR GIRL

DECOY PATTERN

BIG PUFF

READY TO RUT

MILE HIGH SEAT

THE STALKER

THUNDERSTRUCK

A FRESHLY LAID SOD

READY FOR STUFFING

WELL
MOUNTED...

THE WHIP

STUD FARM

ON THE SCENT

BITCH PACK

DRAG HUNTING

DOUBLE BRIDAL

GONE TO GROUND

JUMPING DYKES

FOXY LADY

BREAKING COVER

ROD AND TACKLE...

SPORTING EQUIPMENT

YOU'VE GOT SOME LOVELY TACKLE

CAN I LOOK AT YOUR FLIES PLEASE?

DOUBLE HANDED ROD

KNOTLESS FISHNETS ARE OBLIGATORY

113

ACTUALLY HE'S GOT A TIDDLER

TAKING A LEAK

FISHING WITH A WET FLY

NEVER MIND, THEY SAY SIZE DOESN'T MATTER

FISHNETS

BOTTOM FEEDER

FISHING CAMP

HOOKED

NO NYMPHS BEFORE AUGUST

WHAT A WHOPPER!

COARSE FISHERMAN